Finger V

GW01388456

Poetry as Re

Hughie Carroll

Foreword

What I love about "Finger Writing" is Hugh's humility, delight, compassion and insight into life's heartfelt yet comedic moments – his focus on glimmer.

I love how his words paint a loving brush-stroke sketch of the trials and tribulations of daily life, to which we can all relate.

In studying "Finger Writing" in preparation for writing this foreword, I have noticed a delightful "Hughishness" shift in how I see the world; and my willingness to highlight and expand on such glimmer moments, and to think of the words I would use to portray them.

I recently took some training in how to calm the central nervous system, as a tool for health, clarity, and measured response. I was invited to roam around outside looking for glimmer: be it something beautiful, funny, or sad....something that lights you up inside; then to describe it to a another person. Apparently this practice of focus on glimmer, to seek it out, pay it attention, and to invite expansion of the sensory feelings it engenders; this gradually retrains the brain to a greater awareness of glimmer, thus inviting more magic and delight into daily life. Much in the same way that meditation does, this practice seems to act as a soothing, healing balm for the central nervous system, which in these modern times can so often be over-stimulated and stuck in a jangly, frazzled mode.

Ah Hugh, what a journey your life has been so far: Computer geek, Buddhist monk, carer, phenomenal juggler and magician, ace guitarist, circus performer, kite flyer, mindfulness teacher, poet, survivor.

Hugh has that rare ability to turn his hand to anything and be outstanding at it. Let us never forget that Hugh's song (to me, all of his poems are different verses of his life's song) pivots around one traumatic event when he fell from a great height whilst rehearsing in the circus. He actually died for a period of time, and was surprised to wake up back on planet earth with life-changing injuries. Post injury life style allows plenty of time for reflection on glimmer, past and present.

What if we ARE put on this earth primarily to play? To revel in glimmer? To love and laugh?

Thanks for the Poems Hugh, King of the Glimmer.

Kate Verney
Body Harmony teacher
Retired Circus clown and wirewalker

Preface

The title poem 'Finger Writing' comes from the symbol of water vapour condensing into droplets when it meets a plate of cold glass which is quite a bit like the process of writing. Amorphous ideas, emotions, sentiments, 'condense' into ink marks on the surface of the page or screen. In addition, when you write on a steamed up window pane with your finger you are usually pointing, quite literally, at your own reflection. How pleasing for an image to speak so eloquently! We see ourselves reflected in our attempts at self-expression. Half seen, half remembered fragments swimming about in the unconscious come up and make themselves known.

There are the usual anecdotes, some jokes, philosophising and musing, but all the pieces are 'waited for' rather than forced. I've been trying to avoid deliberately poetic devices in the main, they are added here and there admittedly, but overall I've waited and listened to the unconscious as far as I'm able and eventually something comes up.

Hughie
September 2024

<u>finger writing</u>

droplets condensed
on a window
moments ago
they were vapour

free

a hard surface
freezes words
into black and white

finger writing
on glass
I point
at my reflection

<u>book</u> <u>worm</u>

the most grown up thing ever
when i was about 7
was walking to the library
filling in a form
getting a card
and choosing a book
Sherlock Holmes
or Tolkein maybe
and reading all the stories
every last one

ah the thrill
of escape
into other worlds
like dandelion clocks
drifting through time
little word packets
found a home
in me

taking a book back
when the library lady
stamped the return date
something like
joy victory wonder
deeply intoxicating
surged through my wee body
and made me believe
that just maybe
life was going to be
ok

solstice

a Glastonbury solstice
near dawn
a young guy
balanced on top
of a standing stone
at the mini-henge
amongst the crowds
awaiting the sacred moment
trying to have
some kind of "pagasm"

he had rainbow laces
in multi-coloured dockies
purple macrame flares
plaited leather belt
paisley waistcoat
with grass leafs
loads of beads
a big felt Dr Seuss hat
and a mahoosive spliff
everything looked
brand new

I looked on
with a bunch of loafers
as someone made a remark
about the poor guy's awkwardness
his self-conscious determination
to have an epic moment

and we cynics
began to take the piss

I recall hysteria breaking out
merciless laughter
people howling
and rolling on the grass
one guy
lying on his back
drummed his feet on the ground
and cried
"no more! no more!"
I hadn't laughed like that
in ages
the fact that he was
only just out of earshot
made it funnier still

all these decades later
with evening coming on
a twinge of shame
has replaced that mirth
a cynical carapace
hasn't defended us
from diddly squat

neither his hopefulness
naivety or pretence
nor our scorn
or street-wise posturing
as we waited

for our suns
to rise
could delay
our fates
blazing
sputtering forth
towards the setting
of that sun

<u>youth</u> <u>c</u>lub

we'd not done a show
together before
me and Dik

a famously rough
council high-rise
booked us
for their youth club

we were given
a little cubbyhole
some tiny store room
to get ready in
about one hundred kids
mostly black
under fourteen-ish
were making
rowdy noises
as we stepped out

around the stage area
stood four or five of them
facing out
towards the crowd
arms folded
being the law

a pang of apprehension
to realise

these tots
needed security

we probably juggled
and might've unicycled
clowning around
but it was a surprise
to me
as much as them
when Dik
did his escapology routine

he produced chains
and locks
and had volunteers
to bind him up
and put him
in a sack

there was a countdown
backwards from ten
as he struggled on the floor

they went ballistic
as we got to
"three two ONE!"
and Dik burst out
wearing nowt
but a posing pouch
sequins glittering
around his bits

and still
all chained up

pandemonium broke loose
people shouting
and rushing forwards
the guards shoved back
some people fell
and so we legged it
back to the cubbyhole
afraid

a forest
of juvenile hands
banged on the glass
with much shouting
and general uproar
as we hastily
put on our street clothes

the mini bouncers
escorted us out
we made the street
and legged it once again

around the corner
we slowed down
and turned back
hearing a high
little boy voice
a wee head

popped around the corner
and called out

"we liked you really!"

clench

a centre had an open day
they hired us for a show
thirty odd teenage boys
all with Down's Syndrome
they were tremendous
and we got off
to a flying start

suddenly

in walked Miss Wales
in full regalia
sash and tiara
and unspeakably
heart-stoppingly
gorgeous

the guys were already lairy
but in her presence
they lost their minds

we invited her
to volunteer
we would knock a cigarette
out of her mouth
with flying juggling clubs
it's a very old trick
all the jokes and patter
well rehearsed

with clubs whistling past
front and rear
she had to stand

still

we asked her
to keep her hands
by her sides
and told her
"if you're going to laugh
do it sideways"
in a brainwave
I asked her
to clench
her buttocks

she was a great sport
and so she did
just to prove it
she turned around
and showed the guys
"one, two, clench!"

it was like a cartoon
the way they went
completely
and utterly

bananas

Noel Reilly

on a slow afternoon in the Beehive
I was working behind the bar
when this red-faced woman
came storming in

"I demand to see the manager!
I live next door
and one of your customers
has just been
outrageously rude to me!"

"Of course Madam
please follow me"
so off we went to the back

I knocked on Noel's door
"What is it?"
he called from upstairs
so I told him
of the upset neighbour

bump bump bump
he came stumping down the stairs
"I'll not be having
my neighbours insulted"
he says
as he opens the door

"THAT'S HIM!"

she shouts
and points right at him
as Noel does a quick 180
and disappears
scuttling back upstairs

<u>Chris</u> <u>Evans</u>

whose name did I write?

now, I don't think I looked
anything like him
Chris Evans that is
him who married Billie Piper
the singer from Swindon

back in the mid 90s
it seemed like you would see
his gingery hair
and thick-rimmed NHS glasses
every time you turned on a TV

this was back before the internet
imagine that!
back when if you wanted
to watch a film at home
you'd have to hire a VHS video

and so it was
that me and my then girlfriend
went to a Blockbusters
in Gorse Hill
to get a copy of True Lies
or was it Pulp Fiction?
anyway
that detail got drowned out
by what happened next

on our way in
some youths on a bench
noticed my characteristics
the gingery hair
the thick-rimmed NHS glasses
and called out 'Chris Evans'
they all laughed
I rolled my eyes
and tutted

in the shop
while we were browsing
there was some banging
on the window
which I ignored
but by the time we came out
a reasonable sized crowd
had formed outside

a bunch of people rushed at us
multiple voices lifted
'Chris Evans'
'Chris Evans'

I couldn't raise my eyebrows
any higher
when someone thrust out
a paper and pen
and asked for an autograph
nearly thirty years later
I honestly can't remember

whose name
I wrote

the under geek

I am
the under geek
no longer cracking the whip
technologies befuddled me
the labyrinth wins and I'm lost
battling to move into brainy spaces
after such a physical youth
perhaps it's time
to let the machines win
and do what I do best

to listen to birds
to hold the impossible scale
of all the suffering
inside my chest
to just allow
all the death struggles
to continue their dying

Danny Boy

Michael's only words
were 'yeah!'
and 'nuh!'
enough to hear
his Irish brogue

the stroke
had been severe

his eyes
always sparkled
with mischief
he'd shuffle over
and do his thumbs up
over and over
forever finding
something to laugh about

at the height of summer
we had a group outing
to Savernake forest
the van had special rails
in the floor
to fasten the wheelchairs

he did his 'yeah!'
and his thumb
to nearly everything
it was marvellous

we had to stay
on the paved path
mostly
until there was a slope
I stood on the back brackets
for a bit
and the two of us
free-wheeled
he laughed so hard
I got carried away
and went again
picking up too much speed
until we spilled out
in a dramatic crash
we were far enough away
from the rest of the gang
to get away with it
but my God
we were nearly sick
laughing

'yeah!'
'yeah!'
(thumb)

on the way home
everyone went quiet
looking out
at the hard yellow summer
minds in neutral
looping with the swifts

and then Michael sang!

really sang
like a chorister
a bell like voice
perfect

'Oh Danny Boy
The pipes the pipes are calling'

everyone's mouths fell open
by the time he got to
'from glen to glen
and down the mountain side'
I felt the tears prickle

but when he sang
'in sunshine or in shadow'
the heart gave way

he sang for all of us

beep

the command I typed
had a space
where it should not have been
a message was supposed
to pop up
on my mate's monitor
it said
"om mani padme hum"
just for something to type
given our conversations
about Buddhism

we sat in a long row
modern day scribes
at computers
the room had dozens of rows
and the message
did arrive
"beep!"
it went

but then the first row
all beeped too
then the second
and so on
sweeping down the room
an electronic wave
of punishment beepings
apparently it went on

to nearly five thousand machines
across the whole company
on multiple sites
around the country

I had changed the message
at the last moment
from
"shave my back
and call me Edna!"

I didn't get sacked
but man
I thought I was having
a heart attack

clickery tappery
is no way
to earn a living

big wig

the big wig explained
just how very big
his bigness really was
power-pointing his way
through charts and numbers
apparently proving
spectacular successes
a God of code
a titan of acumen

when he came into a room
everyone shut up
and fixed their eyes
on their screens

he would stride past
bigly
and if we remained
unfired
someone would sing
the Darth Vader theme
"daaan daaan daaan
dun derdaaan
dun derdaaan"

we felt the relief of rabbits
when the tiger passes by
in search
of bigger game

his big meeting
in the big hall
turned out
to be a valediction
he had been removed
effectively sent
to Siberia
the levers of power
exchanged
for the straightening
of paper-clips

he finished
his big hurrah
and closed his laptop
tucked it under his arm
and paced away
no-one
made eye contact

apart from a slight squeaking
from his shoes
he left
in pin-drop silence

suddenly
my heart went out to him
what is it
to pretend to rule the world
and be
friendless?

top dogs

the top dogs
our chief exec from Murca
with his consigliere
gathered the pack
to throw us a bone
and to tell
of the year's results
the usual damn lies
and statistics

awooooooooooooo!

in question time
I raised my hand
"the bonus scheme
is supposed to motivate us
but the bigger the salary
the bigger the percentage
ensuring nearly everyone
feels hacked off!
how about
just give a flat rate?
you spend the same
and nearly everyone
would feel great!"

"that's not the world
we live in"
barked the number two

"don't we make the world
with our decisions?"
I asked

they left it hanging
as a rhetorical question

a few days later
I saw the number two
in a corridor
he sniffed me out
and whispered
conspiratorially
"that lefty rubbish
won't wash with me!"

yes they get the lion's share
but
the dog-eat-dog mind
belongs to the animals

Negev

I was about to tell him the tale
of that time doing a show
someone jumped too soon
and I took off into the night sky
holding on with finger tips
some sixty feet above the stage
there was only the briefest moment
to get my hands back in the straps
so I could break my fall
upside down my mind took
a snapshot
the Negev desert
the crowd of eight thousand
the lights on the stage
far far below
etched in the memory
raw terror
raw life
but he stopped me
right at the start
and said
"there's no story
you can possibly tell
that I can't top"

kite

lifting spinning
breezy flitting
kite strings sing
whipping wind whistles
words flew
right out
of my head

gotta die

(song lyrics)

cancer pneumonia
HIV
choking on a bun
with your cup of tea
tripping on the carpet
falling down the stairs
the light turns red
catch you unawares

everybody's gotta die
but we're still alive

fall from the ladder
and your back is broke
the house catches fire
you go up in smoke
your arteries are furred
you block a ventricle
an ovary a lung
a breast a testicle

everybody's gotta die
but we're still alive

thrown from the train
stabbed in the back
you lend your kidneys to a friend
and you don't get 'em back
a heart attack a stroke

the wrong injection
take viagra
get a fatal erection

everybody's gotta die
but we're still alive

the perils of life
are crowding in upon us
don't sit on my lap
if you're a hippopotamus
it started with a kiss
and ended up in homicide
nothing seemed amiss
except a certain whiff of cyanide

everybody's gotta die
but we're still alive

dangle from a rope
a hand-full of pills
slipping on the ice
the winter kills
we all gotta die
we're all on the clock
reach 98 and your

heart

just

stop

pretend

why do junkies always
tell you that they're clean
and pillars of society
turn out the most obscene
the friends who fawn with flattery
and smiles a mile wide
it's them that stab you in the back
they've got the most to hide
we've all constructed facades
but falsities offend
don't they say let's all be nice
so pretend pretend pretend

tricks

impromptu magic show
a large Indian family
had reacted with fear
it was a shock
to see
how they really believed
it was something supernatural
I toyed with the feeling
such awesome potential
but soon gave up
the temptation
and showed them
how some of it was done
"look, it's in the other hand!"
they relaxed
and began to have fun
it was a relief
yes there's a deception
but the intent is to charm
to amuse
to bridge the gap
but they are right
to be afraid
look at these other deceptions
the ones that lead
to lynchings
to concentration camps
the appalling trick
of stirring up rage

of summoning demons
like the fear of foreigners
or the belief in superiority
I walked away from the family
but paused
a little boy tried some magic
all by himself
he held a stone
and closed his hand
he blew on it
just as I had done
he snapped his fingers
just like me
and opened his hand
only to find the stone
still there!
his eyes went as wide
as they could go
his mouth
perfectly round
he really learned it
that time
that it wasn't real
not like those others
those who believe
their own sorcery
that they are victims
even while
they kill

itself

John I still miss you
but not so much
especially now I've remembered
our last interview
we gazed into each other's eyes
for a time out of time
where I can see you again
any time I like
in that eternal present
in silent appreciation
of this moment
just being itself

bins

the expanse of sky

so clear

so empty

the evening

cool and massive

suddenly happy

putting out the bins

another birthday

minutes often drag
but decades are whipping by

what is this "time"
that people
keep talking about?

<u>Thursday</u> <u>boys</u>

up the boozer
my mates

the pulse of friendship
outpacing marriages
and careers

easy come easy go
beer and banter
on girls
and physics
and

bicycles

bicycles

bicycles

<u>snow</u> <u>ball</u>

the snow was brilliant
the whole school
going mad
the play ground riotous
snow balls flying everywhere

Sister Mary
in full habit
came to break it up
blowing her whistle
and shoo-ing everyone
back to their classes

as we left
I turned to see her
shoving the boys
off the other side
of the playground

one last snow ball
might just reach her
what was that?
fifty yards or something?
I don't know

like magic
it left my hand
and described the perfect arc
never before or since

have i thrown such a throw

even now
I recall the apalling thrill
the sheer jubilation
the back of her head
protected by a dark blue veil
went 'dufff'

thirst

it was thirst

that drove the iceberg

to drift across the seas

searching for its source

even as it melted

away

(for Kathy)

don't freak out

when Hughie is freaking out
Cháng Kè says:
ruminating on hurts of the past
only hurts you in the present
it's usually pain and tiredness
that is really the problem
so stop trying to figure it out
stop trying to fix it
stop trying

it's only a false alarm
remember your heart
is both good and true
and is made up out of
everything and everyone else
and so practice
is for all of us

the universe wants you
or you wouldn't be here
your honour is redeemed
the pain is not failure
it's the fare for the ferryman
to bring you back across
just what Mother Nature needs
in return for your life
so have a rest
then take the backward step
love cannot arrive from outside

we must return
in silent appreciation
to this moment
just being itself
and sit still
in the heart
with all suffering beings

have faith and surrender
to the surrounding hush
so bright
with loving

rhyme

The practice of poetic rhyming,
Of rhythm and metre and timing,
Are rules you can follow
or

not

deluge

above the waterline
we speak
and breathe
an airy world
where we think
we are
where lightness
loving bright
reaches
for nobility

below the waistline
slow motion
deaf unsteady
wading heavy
primal urges
heaving up
sex
and murder
sinking mutely
into shit

the deluge comes
regardless
so speak
while you can
and take a stand
while there is yet
ground
beneath your feet

shoes

argument and counter-argument
all night long
the philosophers debated
locking horns over free will
wrestling
about karma

after every hair was split
at last the morning came
and so
tired out
and none the wiser
the unstoppable force
and the immovable object
got up and left

which shoe each of them
put on first?

that was free will

the second?

karma

words

little time capsules
propelled into futures
and returning
from vagueness

words

i bet you don't remember
writing us
but here we are
reminding you

centred
in amazing chaos
you are ablaze
with the mystery

oh yes
the very same
nothing less
the mystery
of forever

ink

popping the lid
on a violent heaven

ink
squiggles off the stick

bone ivory
annihilating into
cerulean blue
becoming sky
its aroma
intoxicating
a vibration
you can breathe

iris widens
pure magenta
cyan conjuring
with indigo
and jade

somehow eyes feel
the frequencies
down to the feet
redolent
with memory

summer's goldenrod boyhood yellow

September's burnt melancholy ochre

violet's first amethyst kiss

red's primal scarlet uproar

midnight's longing blue quiet

forest's calm emerald pulse

the ink by itself
was always more exciting
than any shapes they made
on paper

<u>30</u> years

thirty years ago

today

that young man died

three decades of mourning

this old man

still struggling

to be born

some days

some days
the pain won't stop
and sleep
won't come

some days
are just going
to be like that

some days
all the stories
about love
and its triumph
over death
just won't wash

some days
everything
makes you cry

when death whispered
in my ear
when death
shouted down the house
I hoped
it might make me
special somehow

but some days
I realise
no-one really
wants to hear
about the end

ghost

the death was years ago
my God how long has it been?
decades anyway
I don't know
when the anniversary comes around
i get increasingly tense
in the few weeks before
and often wonder
why i can't remember
the funeral

so how do i fill these days?
hard to say
hard to describe
a nondescript drifting
a groping through greyness
a searching
for something to satisfy
a seeking
after something real

there are tons of stories
that make it sound
all glamorous and sexy
about being dead
but mostly
it's really boring

mostly
all the philosophising
is inconclusive

thoughts and feelings
still keep happening
but i'm not sure
who they are happening to
exactly

is it the guy who fell?
there was a sudden rush
into blackness
a confrontation
with the abyss

maybe it was the woman?
she rushed to help
and cradled a body
forgetting
they were supposed
to have split up

or the other guy perhaps?
sore rope-ripped hands
sprinting for help
on painful feet

both those guys
loved that woman
she loved the fallen one

but they fought
way too much
to stay together
all that scene
is on the other side
of a veil
where things happened
to characters
who had actual lives
a place
where people knew each other
and often said things like
"hi!"
and "what's that?"
and "i love you!"

i miss it
but if i'm honest
i can't expect people
to talk to me
when i'm invisible

leaking

the cabin boy said
"my God, the ship is leaking"

the captain said
"put him in irons
he is a hypocrite
weighing us down
like everyone else"

the optimists
along with the pessimists
the doomsters
and activists

drowned

stick

walking stick
on the conveyor belt
at the airport

the official
picked it up
and called after
the old couple
who had just left

"I think you've left this"

they turned back
still fiddling
with belts
and jackets

this was the moment
that I had dreaded

"the stick is mine"

all three
looked at me

mute
I still thought of myself

as a fuckin' Samurai

I still thought of the stick
as belonging to my dad

it's not a katana
sssssssik
with its rubber ferrule
thomp thomp

my cheeks burned
with a clamour
I couldn't name
as I thomp
thomped away

<u>two</u> <u>wheeled</u> <u>tiger</u>

we somehow acquired
a clapped out motorbike
a washing up liquid bottle
for a fuel tank
front brake lever repurposed
as a throttle

the engine actually ran
it was very exciting
but the time spent
naming it "the tiger"
and painting it with stripes
would've been better spent
fixing its saddle

at last they gave me a go
on nearby parkland
instructions were given
right brake lever
go
left brake lever
stop
I don't recall
if gears were involved
such details drowned out
by the intoxication
of the burbling motor

the smell
of popping petrol smoke

by gosh I think I had it
and off I went

bouncing across the grass
the saddle immediately gave way
I slid off the back
the rubber of the back wheel
dangerously close

highly motivated
to keep my boyhood danglies
from being erased
I spontaneously demonstrated
the yoga pose known
as "the scorpion"

from such a position
I was unable to release my grip
on the throttle

weeeeeeee!

such exertions
had taken my attention
from any notion of steering
as it lurched and bounced
around the grassy banks
far too late

I noticed a young tree
supported by cables
approaching at a bit more
than running speed

my neck proved
heroically tougher
than the diagonal wire
that pinged me backwards

the tiger
had a brief spell
of freedom
before it collapsed
into a heap
and growled

Sam

a brilliant little dog
was our Sam
a feisty Jack Russell

he would sit
with his back legs crossed
aristocratic
aloof
and wait for the railway workers

three times a day
the big siren would sound
haunting
and thousands of Lowry-esque guys
on bicycles
would spill forth
peddling home

Sam's ears would prick
he'd look up the street
and get ready

dozens of legs
going up and down
trying to shuck him off
in his deadly
game of bones

one time he was missing
for days
we got a phone call
that he had been seen
sitting in the middle of the road
over four miles away
traffic streaming both sides
unconcerned
insouciant legs
crossed

blob dog

he was a big bouncy Collie
was Jake
we usually called him
'blob dog'
for some reason
no one could remember

my dad had taken him for a walk
and on their way home
he stopped off
for a newspaper
leaving the blob
in the car

standing in the queue
dad heard a car's horn
blaring
it went on and on
as he inched forward
towards his turn
at the cash desk

at last
getting back to the motor
he found blobby
sitting in the driver's seat
paws on the wheel
looking most
alarmed

guard dog

after the show
laughter applause uproar
echoeing freshly
we packed it all up
putting the tent to bed
everyone wanted to go for a bevvy
all rosy-cheeked and frisky
but we couldn't leave all the gear
unattended
amps and instruments
lights and props
the whole little-big-top

our visitors told of their circus
they had a guard dog
they tied it to the main rope
hanging from the top rigging bar
he could roam around
the centre circle
ready to give the frighteners
to any intruders

so our Jakey-boy
the 'blob'
was duly given the audition
I tied him firmly
gave him a little scriggle

told him he was a good boy
picked my way out
of the darkened tent
and off we jogged
to the pub

at kicking out time
flushed with bonhomie
we wandered back
what was that?
something in the distance?

wooooooooooo awooooooooooo
awoooooooooooooooooooooooooooo

I rushed back
bumped through the scenery
and released blobdog
all alone in the dark
trembling

our mates laughed
"that's no guard dog"
but I felt so guilty
he had tons of extra treats
he was a much nobler creature
than me
I can't forgive that fast
not like a dog can

zebra

Joolz wanted to buy the zebra
it was an actual zebra
stuffed
and standing about weirdly
in the second hand shop
the natural habitat
for terrible taxidermy specimens

the idea had seized her
and our chum Sally
and so it was
that the three of us
went to make the purchase

huh students!

anyway
it turns out it's really hard
to lug about
African equine awkward
and very heavy

there was quite a way to go
and while they announced
amidst gales of laughter
that it was going to be called
Bret

(Bret?)

i decided to lift it
using the classic
fireman's lift

as soon as i got it up
on my shoulders
i legged it
for home

after a quarter of a mile
or so
enduring the honking
of passing cars
i was shagged
so i put it down
and turned back

waaay in the distance
i could just make out
the waving
of arms and legs
as they lay on the floor
in convulsions

homo geologicus

a personality
and a landscape both
collide with the present
only after
a tortuous formation

a laval eruption
of madness
when a straightjacket
of regolith
cracks

sedimentary deposits
pressed down over millennia
into resentful mudstone

bubbling springs
of youthful joy

alluvial meanderings
of maturity

porous limestone labyrinths
carving chemical confusions

our momentary snapshots
of the character of place
take in only the surface

the kaleidoscope of time
delivers to us
just fragments
created over epochs

mica and schist
the granite of high places
brooding over memories
of a fossilised sea

ancient tectonic psychodramas
authority versus rebellion
throw up vast mountains
and arid
icy deserts

nothing could withstand
the glacier's hydrosexual demand
for the ocean

to wear the mantle
as it is
rather than try
to remake a world
is surely
a more graceful way
to honour
its contours

Orion

hanging over the neighbour's roof
Orion
winter's a-comin then
his glittering belt of nebulae
solid proof
of magic

as I gawp
and try to remember
the old names
I twiddle my beard
other hand on hip
and wonder
if some far distant ancestor
had ever done
this exact same thing

just before an Autumn dawn
not sleeping
his dog
having a pee

there!
Menkalinan
Aldebaran
Bellatrix
and just behind the tree
wow!
Rigel!

all a-glitter

maybe too low
to see Sirius
one of the hunter's dogs
only a bazillion miles
the other side
of the shed

the unthinkable reaches
of aeons
of light years
the immeasurable heaven
of Laniakea
all that space
all that time
apparently
the same thing

what a trick!

my tea
will have brewed by now
me and the dog
go back in
he's a pain
but I can't help but love him
lil' Bernie boo
here at the centre
of the cosmos

deep sea shopping

it's pretty hard to see
out of this massive
copper helmet
the breathing
is laboured too
the water pressure
at this depth
is crushing

the folks out shopping
all around
seem to be doing fine

the lead boots
are very hard to lift
and the hangover
from the whisky
is blinding

but I'm wearing
flip flops
and didn't drink
a drop

honest

somehow

while I slept
someone has sandpapered
all my bones
and the fluey ache
just won't quit

when people say
"you're looking well!"
oddly
it doesn't cheer me up
then I remember
they can't see nuffink

they seem fine
which means
I can't see nuffink
either

and so it seems
we only really see
when we listen

currency

they try to turn everything
into a currency
but regardless
time itself will steal it

these markets all thrum
with the commerce
of youth sex power wealth
the turbo charged engines
of desire

your value measured
in the stock exchange
weighed in the balance
of celebrity
algorithms buying and selling
our attention

but what
if anything
remains sacred?

tears?
love?
birdsong?

penalty

we were duffers at footy
but my mate had a penalty
eight or nine years old
school playground

somehow
he managed to half miss
spin around and fall over

the ball lazed away
diagonally backwards

everyone laughed
except Oxley
he flew into a rage
and started kicking
my supine chum
kicking hard too
so I pushed him away
what else?

the red mist had come
but I wasn't ready
he punched me repeatedly
piston like
both hands
in the face

the
feel
of
the
wool
of
his
gloves
on
my
cheek
bones

surprisingly ineffective

I couldn't hit him back
where his piston arms
were pumping
so moving my thumb
over my finger
door knocking position
aimed at his temple
swung round the outside
and connected

the squishy hard impact
didn't feel like much
but down he went
like a dropped towel

curled into a ball

we left him

the footy continued

later he was seen orbitting
around
around
the not so playful
playground
handkerchief to his eyes
head down

"sorry Hughie"
he said
when the bell rang

mirror-scope

always microscoping

in

to the tiniest of details
they insist
on the basis of things
as physical

mind
coming out
of matter

others telescoping

out

to the grandest of mysteries
insist
on the basis of things
as spiritual

matter
coming out
of mind

still others scope a

mirror

asking
what of the eye

                behind the lens?

what is doing

                the looking?

what of the laughter
when a dog

                farts?

or the worry
about being

                bad?

what of the concern
when a friend gets

                ill?

or the turmoil
about being

                mad?

what of the love

that could embrace a

world?

or the anguish
about being

sad?

do they scry
in their viewfinders
the broken triumph

of an ordinary day?

the abject comedy

of a lifetime?

I gaze bewildered
into this mirror-scope
the gaze itself
is miracle enough

(for Stoo)

dictionary

in a dictionary of missing words
the story of a missing life

the self utters itself
thus a person is narrated
into being

I search the clamour and anguish
of a language not my own
for a true word

Olympus

in the Olympian spotlight
the Gods
youth beauty power
success fame vitality
write a dictionary
that seeks to define us
we've been framed
some of us are cast into shadow
the pages of our own dictionaries
torn out
there are those among these exiles
who turn to face that night
and in their listening
discover a new voice
write their own words
come
add your inky darkness
to ours

breezes

the breezes at play
self-concern dropped
there is no other moment

butterfly

fluttering against glass
the butterfly longs for the garden
an invisible pain

<u>fairy</u> <u>tales</u>

in childhood we believe in demons
in adolescence we wise up
"haha! stupid! they're not real"
and we are consoled for a time
only in later life
after the tears and terrors
the furies of the night
do we return to those fairy tales
and realise how true they are
how meticulously honest
to the ravages of darkness

Lally & Tom

Aunty Lally was a star
she had been one of those
boat pushers
on the big maps
in the war room
second world war that is

in the old black & white movies
those model boat pushers
are all young and sexy women
in uniforms
with those boxy caps
with black peaks

Uncle Tom took a shine to her
and said he'd marry her
straight off
so the family story goes

I'd see them periodically
as I grew up
I loved Big Tom's pipe smoke smell
and Aunty Lally's exotic red lipstick

they were filled with secrets
of the Bletchley Park sort
or so I imagined
all Douglas Bader
and derring do

also the terrible umbra
of tragedy
haunted from the shadows
Johnny their son
had died
crashing a mini
like Mark Bolan

when Big Tom died
he was buried near his son
as we left the cemetery
the guys were ready
with a gravestone
I asked to have a look
leaning over the flat-bed trailer
I read
"He danced the sky
On laughter silvered wings" (*)
he had been a real life pilot

years later
at another Uncle's house party
Lall plied me with gin
"I do like a young man"
she kept saying
an old lady
with the same red lipstick
mixed with coke
it all seemed like fun
until I got violently
and very publicly

sick

I'm so happy I knew them
and I hope they knew
how much I loved them

it was long after
they'd both gone
I suddenly noticed
the spelling of my name "Hugh"
how odd

at last I realised
why Tom had always called me
"Hoo, How or Huff"

locusts

the heat on my face
from the locust box
was like being there
in that imagined desert
hundreds of them
very still
until one would jump
always freaked me out
just a bit
then they would resume
their alert stillness
electric noises
weirdly insect like
in their artificial vivarium

I fed them
following instructions
from the Biology teacher
he had told us
at the start of the course
that it was all about
the study of life
and so I studied them

the stripes on their long bodies
their amazing identical striations
bulbous darkness in their eyes
something both scary
and endearing

I couldn't make it out
their strangeness
captivating

arriving at the next lesson
I found that the teacher
had prepared a dissection
and the locusts
every last little one
were dead

killed in the name
of a bastard science

if this is the study of life
then they will study it
without me

turning on my heel
I silently left
refusing them the respect
of any debate

<u>carpe noctem</u>

slender Sevilla was from Roma
deep brown drowning eyes
black springing ringlets
I fell
in

she made me laugh so hard
Greek delirious night life
last bars closing
let's find
somewhere

cat burgling across ceiling joists
drunken Russians sprawled below
a locked room
damned key
undiscovered

joy back on the street
under a lamp post
orbitted by mosquitos
she had
waited

the Cyclades rocks still warm
radiating summer's ferocious heat
night breezes cooling
grateful limbs
caressed

wandering beachward arm in arm
beyond the street lights
firework stars erupted
slow motion
aloft

our sliding dark interiors commingled
lying on the sand
breath taken plunging
shuddering together
immaculate

racing hearts slowed and soared
gentle waves came reaching
a cradled moment
drifting into
galaxies

our youth not entirely squandered
we seized the night
honouring Aphrodite's grace
with our
yes

tenderness

yes there are voids
gulfs that stretch out

between us

yes there is yearning
to cross over the abyss
to delve down
to common ground

yet aren't we strangely together
in this untouched isolation
of tenderness?

Index: <u>Finger</u> <u>Writing</u>

Other works by the author:

Yarn: Selected Poems
Sunshine & Shadow: Poems on Living
Mahabodhi Moonlight (travelogue)
Thesium (sci-fi)

Lots more on https://hugle.uk